Hacking for Beginners:

The Complete Guide

Tim Barnes

Furthermore, the transmission, duplication or reproduction of any of the following work including specific information will be considered an illegal act, irrespective of if it is done electronically or in print. This extends to creating a secondary or tertiary copy of the work or a recorded copy and is only allowed with express written consent of the Publisher. All additional right reserved.

The information in the following pages is broadly considered to be a truthful and accurate account of facts, and as such any inattention, use or misuse of the information in question by the reader will render any resulting actions solely under their purview.

There are no scenarios in which the publisher or the original author of this work can be in any fashion deemed liable for any hardship or damages that may befall them after undertaking information described herein.

Additionally, the information in the following pages is intended only for informational purposes and should thus be thought of as universal. As befitting its nature, it is presented without assurance regarding its prolonged validity or interim quality. Trademarks that are mentioned are done without written consent and can in no way be considered an endorsement from the trademark holder.

Table of Contents

Introduction

Congratulations on downloading this book and thank you for doing so.

The following chapters will explain to you how you can go from knowing nothing about hacking to learning the basics that you will need to know to get started.

There are plenty of books on this subject on the market, thanks again for choosing this one! Every effort was made to ensure it is full of as much useful information as possible, please enjoy!

Chapter 1: What You Need to Know

If you have never done any work with hacking in the past, or you have no experience with it, there are a few things that you will need to know to make sure that you are doing things the right way and that you are able to get them done so that you can get the most out of the hacking experience. There is a lot of information that you will need to learn before you are even able to start learning about the different languages and scripts that you can use, but learning this will go quickly.

The most important thing to learn is that there are different types of hackers. There are ones who are able to do things for good, for bad, and for reasons that nobody but them knows about. Learn a little about each of the types of hackers so that you will know which type you want to be (and which you don't want to be).

Black Hat

These are the hackers that you are probably used to hearing about in the news and in movies. They are the ones who break into systems, ruin computers, and steal your information. Despite the fact that these are the most "popular" type of hackers, they represent only a small percentage of the entire hacking population, and they are generally something that you may not even come into contact with on a regular basis while you are hacking. It is a good idea to make sure that you *know* about these types, though, because they are really the biggest problem that you will eventually have to look out for.

Many people do not aspire to be a black hat hacker. They only want to be a hacker, but they end up caught in this trap because it is something that they think that they are doing for the right reasons or they think that it will not cause much harm. Some hackers may not have a choice and may be forced to use black hat tactics because of a perilous financial situation or because they are being directed to by the person who has shown them how to hack. No matter how they got there, most of the black hat hackers did not start out by intentionally wanting to be a "bad" hacker.

White Hat

If you have ever used someone to help you get a virus off of your computer, someone who can control the computer from a remote location, or someone who can help you protect against the "bad" hackers, you have already had contact with a white hat hacker. Many people choose to be hackers because they want to help people and they know that being a white hat is the way to do it. They set out to go against all of the black hat hackers, and they work to make sure that the people who they serve are able to get the help that they need when it comes to different hacking situations.

It is important to note that the majority of people who are white hat hackers do not work on their own. They work for companies or corporations who are able to use their services to protect their own assets, to market their services to people who come to them, and to allow the chance to make sure that they are getting the best protection possible.

There are some white hat hackers who work on their own, but it is more difficult for them to find work because so few people know about them or what they are able to do to make things better.

Script Kiddie

A Script Kiddie is anyone who steals the codes that others have written and uses them for some type of black hat hacking.

Some hackers who *do* start out with the intention of being bad or doing things that are illegal will start out as Script Kiddies. They often do not even stay in the business of hacking for very long because they only want to use other people's work. They have no aspiration to make up their own codes or their own information, and that can be a problem because there is only so much copying that they can do until they have run out of codes to use.

The Script Kiddies are among the most disliked in the hacking community. White hat hackers dislike them, black hat hackers dislike them also. Even the N00bz, if they knew what they were, would dislike the Script Kiddies. They take away from the good work that all of the white hats are trying to do while also stealing the work that the black hats have done with the malicious scripts they have written. Whether you are trying to learn hacking or not, try your hardest not to be a Script Kiddie.

N00b

Everyone who is in hacking started out as a noob. Whether you are planning on being a good hacker or a bad hacker, you will be a noob until you learn the ropes. If you have a good teacher who can show you everything that you need to know about hacking, you will not be an n00b for too long but, no matter what, you should make sure that you are working to learn everything that you need to know as quickly as you possibly can.

For the most part, the community is nice to n00bz. As long as you are learning and you do not get too overly confident with yourself or become narcissistic about your hacking skills, most people will be willing to help you. The community is always open to helping out others who are hacking for the right reason, who want to make a difference in the world and who want to become a part of something that is so much bigger than what others have done up until that point.

Most people who read the descriptions usually have a good idea of what they want to be and the type of hacker they are going to start out as. This is because many people want to be white hat hackers and, surprisingly, most do not have much interest in learning how to do bad things when it comes to hacking. Make sure that you are doing the right thing with hacking and that you are able to get the most out of it by deciding first what you want to be, how you want to do it, and who you want to be able to help. After you have decided what type of hacker you are going to be, you should learn some of the few key terms to hacking.

All of these terms are things you will come across while you are hacking and you should make sure that you know them. It is a good idea to print off the glossary and keep track of it so that you know what information you are looking at. If you do not want a hard copy of it, just make sure that you save it somewhere you will know about later on.

Spam –

This is used by black hat hackers to get information from people or to cause them to get a virus on their computer. It is used on social media, emails and other types of messages. If someone clicks on the spam or puts any of their information in, they will have given their information to a black hatter or will have a virus installed on their computer. Spam has been around for as long as hacking has been.

Remote Access –

This is controlling a computer (or anything else) from a different location that is ... *remote!* There are many reasons for this, both good and bad. Black hat hackers use this to be able to take over a person's computer for bad reasons and to bring harm to the computer. White hat hackers are able to use this to help a person fix their computer or get rid of any malware that may have come from black hat hackers.

Hacking –

Taking away from the way that the computer is supposed to operate. Changing it by using codes and other information that will allow you the chance to make things look different on your computer. It can be used for both good and bad, but is most commonly used for good.

It is, essentially, manipulating a computer to do exactly what you want it to do.

Firewall –

Many computers have these in place, and they are supposed to help keep a hacker from getting through the computer and able to hack into it. The problem with the majority of firewalls is that they provide a false sense of security. Beyond n00bz and Script Kiddies, nearly every hacker is able to get past most firewalls. These are mostly useless unless the program that is trying to get into the computer is an actual program instead of just a hacker who wants in.

Doxing –

This happens when someone becomes exposed online and is something that will allow you the chance to see that you are dealing with a bad person. Doxing is usually something that black hat hacker use but it can also be used for others on someone who is doing something bad. Doxing usually occurs in online communities where there is anonymity. The hacker will get the information, like the IP address, personal name, and other identifying information, and expose the person in an online scenario. This can be physically dangerous to the person who is being doxed.

Trojans –

Think of the Trojan horse. This is one big file that has many small files inside that can be malicious. The big file is often downloaded because the person who does it thinks that it is harmless. It usually has a different name and is something that seems innocent.

Spyware –

If you want to see what someone is doing on their computer all the time, you will need spyware. The most common use of spyware is to help people get their computer fixed and running correctly, but it can also be used maliciously for people who want to learn about the different things that are on a person's computer. It can be really detrimental if you have unwanted spyware on your computer.

Code –

This is the information that will dictate what you write about and the information that you include in different things. It translates from different symbols and letters to actual, readable text that will show people what you are talking about. Codes are used by hackers, as well as script writers.

Bots –

Computer generated hacker. Hackers may make bots to help them do tasks. The biggest benefit of a bot is that it is automated and you do not need a computer operator to be able to use the bot. They are great for people who want to be able to automate processes. Cortana, Siri, and Alexa are just a few of the most famous bots.

Malware –

Anything that is put on a computer that is meant to bring harm to the computer or the person using it is malware. This is a term that is used for everything from traditional viruses to Trojans and everything in between. If the program is put on the computer to bring harm, then it is malware.

Keystrokes –

When you type, this is a keystroke. Each time that you write a "letter," there is a keystroke that responds to it. There are many reasons for keeping track of keystrokes, but the majority of black hat hackers do this so that they are able to get passwords or private information.

Hacktivist –

Anyone who is hacking for a cause is a hacktivist. This is something that will make people have a different opinion of the hacker and will change the way that the hacker is able to react to different things. There are many options for hackers who want to hack with a cause, but the majority of people do it for social or political purposes. Many do it to help take down corruption and problems that come along with the government or other social establishments.

No matter what you learn about hacking, keeping these key terms in mind will help you become a better hacker and avoid different things. If you are a white hat hacker, you will need to learn these terms because they will likely be things that you are trying to fix for people or trying to get rid of before they have a chance to make a negative impact.

Chapter 2: White Hat Hacking

Even with the basic knowledge that you have learned about hacking, in addition to information that you may already know, there are some things that will make a difference for you when it comes to hacking for good reasons. You should make sure that you are aware of what you can do to make sure that you are getting what you need out of hacking. There are many problems that you may come across, but remember all of these things will help you to remember your initial goal — to be a white hat hacker.

As you go through this chapter, try to find something that you did not already know. The chances are that there is quite a bit that you didn't know and you will be able to use this information to help yourself out. There is a lot more information in each of the following chapters, but this information focuses mostly on white hat hacking and how you can do it.

It Looks Average

Whether you are a white hat hacker or a black hat hacker, you really don't need to worry about those malicious looking black screens with bright green writing. They are rarely used when it comes to hacking, and they are actually pretty bad for your eyesight, so don't even think about that when you are considering becoming a hacker.

The chances are that you will be looking at something that looks very similar to your desktop on a daily basis. This is because hacking usually involves files and moving things around on the computer instead of trying to put the code into word processing systems. This is, perhaps, one of the biggest misconceptions that people have about hacking. The way that hacking is perceived in movies is much different from what it really is in real life, and you are more likely to see bright colors and your favorite desktop background than you are to see an old computer with lines of confusing codes.

Ethical Hacking

There are many different types of ethical hacking, and they can mean something different to each person who is a hacker. This is because there is no exact black and white when it comes to hacking. Yes, it is wrong to hack into someone's bank account and get their information to remove the money. But, is it so wrong if that person had originally stolen thousands of dollars from other people?

To be able to be a successful white hat hacker, you need to make sure that you have a strong moral code and that *you* know what you are comfortable with. It is all about making sure that you are within your own comfort zone and you are getting what you need out of hacking each time that you do it. If not, the hacking will not be worth it, and you may have to worry about the problems that come along with ethical inconsistencies.

Try Not to Bring Bad

Most ethical hackers work with the idea that they will do everything that they can to keep people out of harm's way. This means that they do not bring malicious software into computers no matter what the reason would be for. They also try to keep privacy in mind most of the time. If they can avoid it at all, they will do everything that they can to not put spyware or anything else on the computer that could be detrimental.

By trying your best to bring no harm to people who you work with or for, you will be able to make sure that you are as ethical as possible about your hacking. This is the most common area that white hat hackers go bad in. They do not know when to stop, and they begin to bring harm to other people with their hacking skills.

Test it Out

Whether you are making a code for yourself, for someone else or for a company that you may work for, you need to always make sure that you are testing it out before you put it into action. There are ways that you can do this and programs that you can download, but no matter how you do it, it needs to be done the right way.

If you are making sure that you do it the right way, you will allow yourself the chance to always have the right hacking and the right codes that come along with it. This is something that can be done easily, and it is just an important step.

If you do not test the hack that you have created, you could risk damaging your own computer or, even worse, someone else's computer.

Learn What You Need

Before you even get started with hacking, you need to learn as much as you possibly can about the different things that you will need to do to be able to hack correctly. Learn some of the codes that you are going to use, try the basics out and move on to new things. Keep a log of everything that you are going to use while you are hacking so that you will be able to do more with it later on. There are many great things that come along with hacking so keeping track of the different codes that you can use will allow you the chance to make sure that you are getting the most out of it.

If you learn what you need before you start actually hacking, you will be one step ahead of the other n00bz who may not know what they are doing, and you will be able to make sure that you can truly do your best with hacking when you start out.

Software Downloads

There are some software programs that you will need to be able to effectively hack later on. Make sure that you are aware of these programs and that you have them on your computer so that you will be able to get the most out of them. Doing this will allow you the chance to have the best start possible. It will also give you one less thing that you will need to worry about with hacking when you first start out.

Try different things and different programs. Depending on what you want to do with hacking, you will need several different programs on your computer before starting out with the different things that you can do with it.

Find a Teacher

The easiest way to start hacking is to find someone who will be able to mentor you and help you out with the different things that you need when it comes to hacking. Make sure that the person who you use to help you is someone who knows what they are talking about. There can be problems that come along with hacking, and you will need a professional or an expert to be able to help you with all of the different problems.

Find someone who you trust, who knows what they are doing, and who is going to be patient with you while you are learning all about hacking. This is the easiest way for you to make sure that you are getting the most out of the experience and that you are able to make sure that things will be done the right way when you begin to hack on a professional level.

Apply It

There are so many different applications of hacking that you can choose to work in any sector that you want, really. Hackers can do anything from working for themselves to working for the government with the skills that they develop. This is a great opportunity for people who do not have many skills, and hacking is relatively easy to learn if you keep your mind open to all of the possibilities.

Just make sure that you are prepared for what hacking will be able to help you do, and you make sure that you are getting the most out of it.

While you are trying different things with hacking, keep in mind what you are going to do with it later on down the road. There are many different options that you can choose to do with hacking, and you should make sure that you are doing each of them. There are other options that you have when it comes to your hacking experience. Just make sure that you are learning what you can about hacking and that you are getting the most out of the experience each time you learn something new.

Helping Others

Many people who choose to hack do so because they want to be able to help other people. This is something that they want to be able to do and something that they feel passionate about each time that they do it.

You may choose to help people in the form of a program like anonymous or you may want to do other things with hacking. Most of the people who work to be able to help people out on a personal level are the hackers who work independently on their own to be able to do different things.

Working for Business

There are many businesses, especially technology related ones, that will hire hackers to be able to help them out with the different programs that they have. They want to make sure that they are able to compete with the black hat hackers and they do this through the use of white hat hackers. Since there are not many hackers who are available for this kind of work, there are nearly always businesses that are hiring white hat hackers.

Try to find one that is reputable and one that will help you out with the different things that you may need when it comes to hacking and the different options.

Designing Programs

It is not uncommon for hackers to be program designers as well. People who have hacking skills are also able to create software that can be purchased or downloaded for free. The majority of people who are able to do different things with hacking do so with the software and the same type of codes that are used with software. There are many different options.

Whether you want to be able to add different program options to your hacking experience or you want to make sure that you are getting the most from it, you should make sure that you are able to hack as much as possible and that you can design as many programs as you want. Consider even creating software to help yourself get the hacking experience that you need.

Adding Services

Once you have learned how to hack the right way, there are many different services that you can add onto, and it is something that you will need to make sure that you learn about when you practice hacking. It is a good idea to try to make sure that you are getting the most out of the hacking experience and that you are learning as many services as possible for the people who you are helping. The more experience that you have with helping people and the more services you have to offer, the more valuable you will be when it comes to hacking and the different options that you have to offer.

Chapter 3: Speak the Language

As with any other type of advanced computer writing that you may do, you will need to learn the different languages that are used in hacking. These languages are somewhat difficult to learn when you first start out, but once you know them, they are something that you will not likely forget about at any point in your life. As long as you continue to use them for hacking, you will be able to make sure that you are getting the most out of them.

Learning the language is all about the different aspects of it. There are several different options for hacking, and you need to figure out which language is going to be the best for what you want and the different thing that you are going to be able to do with hacking. Just make sure that you learn the right one, and you will be on your way to becoming a great hacker.

Languages

Even though you will likely find that some of the language aspects that are present in hacking are similar to the other types of writing and coding languages, the hacking one is much different. There are some aspects that are taken from HTML and JavaScript, but they are not the same. It can be beneficial to know the other languages that go along with hacking, but you will not necessarily need to learn the languages to be successful with it. If you know HTML or any other type of coding, that will help you, but do not specifically learn them just so you can hack. You don't necessarily need them.

Once you learn the languages that you need to be able to hack different things, you can do a lot more with them than just the basic hacking that you would like to do. There are many different options for hackers that range from creating programs for the computer, to designing different options, to helping prevent the black hat hackers from getting into the computer. As long as you know the hacking language, you will be able to do nearly anything that you want.

Programming

Learning hacking languages will allow you to become a programmer. You may not be able to develop extremely detailed video games or anything like that, but you will be able to make sure that you can do things on the Internet and by using the computer. You can even design software.

By programming different sites with your hacking skills, you will allow them to do different things and can make them more functional for the people who visit the sites. This type of programming is fairly simple to use in that you just need to have a plain text generator, the knowledge of the language and a way to test it out to make sure that it works for your specific programming guide. There are many different options when it comes to the creation of online coding, and you can use each of them for your own hacking experience.

If you want to design programs that can be used on the computer or just on the Internet, you can also do that with your hacking knowledge. While the languages are different, they are similar in that you can make any program that you want. Each of the programs that you use to make the different codes will be different and will be something that you will need to get used to as you learn more about it and the hacking community.

Different

There are different hacking languages that will work differently depending on the situation that you are in and the type of hacking that you want to be able to do. The hacking language that you choose will be dependent on several different things, but the most important will be which type of hacking you are doing. If you are hacking from a remote location or from the same location will be the biggest determining factor and will make things easier on you if you choose the right one.

Despite the fact that there *are* different languages that you can choose from, they are all relatively similar. They are all written with the same base factors in mind, and they are able to make things better for you, depending on what you want to be able to do with them. It is a good idea to try to make sure that you are getting the most out of each of the languages. Some people choose to learn all three of the hacking languages so that they will always be able to use them for their hacking abilities and will not have to learn something new just because they want to try something else out.

TCP

TCP stands for Transfer control protocol. It is something that will allow you to communicate with the different programs that you are using. It is easier to use than any of the other languages, and it gives you a chance to make communication between both the computer and the other people who are helping you with the hack. It can be used on nearly any operating system and is easy to learn. This is the first language that most people learn, and it is something that is similar. TCP is a combination of each of the other two protocols in addition to some extra features.

One of the best things about learning TCP first is that each of the other languages has elements in them that are similar to TCP. If you can learn how to do different hacks and codes with TCP, it will make it much easier for you to do them with UDP and ICMP. There are many different options that come along with each of the languages, and that is something that you will need to keep in mind when you are writing the different codes that are present in the hacking community.

ICMP

ICMP stands for Internet Control Message Protocol. It is the main form of communication that you will use if you are not using TCP and it is something that is intended to be used to be able to communicate. You can send and receive messages, create messages on the Internet, and send out alerts that tell people what you are doing with the different types of hacking that are present in your own system. It is a great option for people who want to learn the simplest hacking language, and it can be helpful for many different applications.

The biggest problem with ICMP is that you are unable to use it for anything other than communication. You cannot write new codes with it, and you will need to make sure that you are getting the most out of it each time that you do something on it. There are many problems with ICMP, but making sure that you keep all of this in mind each time that you deal with it will allow you the chance to make sure that you are getting the most out of it. While it is relatively useless compared to TCP or even UDP, it is something that can help you learn what some of the hacking elements are in each of the languages that you may use.

UDP

UDP stands for User Datagram Protocol. It does not have quite as many elements as TCP, but it does give you good options for including different things with your hacks. There are many of the programs that are included with UDP that are similar to TCP. If you have learned TCP as your first language, you will likely not need to learn much more to be able to follow the UDP aside from specific codes and hacks that will change the way that you do things.

When it comes to UDP, you should learn as much as possible before you try to do it or try to make sure that it works for you. There are many different options that can be different depending on what you want to be able to do so make sure that your UDP languages are as broad as possible. Learning as much as you can about UDP will guarantee that you are getting the most out of it and that you are able to truly appreciate the hacking languages.

Learning all three of the languages is the only way that you will be able to achieve an expert level of hacking and be able to do everything that you need with your different experiences.

Linux

The majority of people who are hackers or choose to use the hacking languages use Linux. This is an easy to use operating system that is not much different from Windows or MAC. It can be installed on nearly any computer and will give you what you need to be able to hack effectively. The benefits of Linux is that it is specifically designed to be able to used for hacking and does not include some of the unneeded features that are included with other operating systems.

It is always a good idea to get Linux because of how simple it is. This will be your best option for starting out and will give you a chance to do as much as possible with the hacking that you are planning on doing. There are many options for hacking and Linux gives you the chance to be able to use each one of them in a way that makes sense for you.

Cain and Abel

Despite the fact that Linux is your best option for hacking and it will be the best program for you to be able to use, you can also use other operating systems. You just need to make sure that each of them will be up to par with what you want to do when it comes to hacking and that you are getting the most out of each of them. It is a good idea to try different things with your programs and see what you are able to do with the operating system that you have been using.

One of the options for people who are not using Linux because they already have Windows or a different operating system is Cain and Abel. This is a program that will allow you the chance to make sure that you are getting the most out of everything with hacking and that you are able to hack effectively. Getting Cain and Abel for your computer is simple and is something that you will be able to do effectively. It is much less expensive and easier than trying to get a Linux operating system when you are first getting started with hacking and not making money from it.

Collection of Information

One of the easiest things that you can try with your new hacking skills and software is collecting information. This can be done through keystroke loggers or any other type of software. It is ideal for anyone who wants to be able to learn about hacking. One of the first things that people do with their hacking skills is collect information. When you know how to do that, you can then expand on all of the other hacking skills that you need to be able to do more with it.

As you learn more about hacking, you will learn different parts of the language. Because you are learning more each time you do a new hack, you will need to first learn the basics. The basic parts of each of the languages are similar, and they will give you a chance to make sure that you are doing the most with your hacking experience. Learn all of the languages, practice on the software and constantly expand your knowledge if you want to be able to be the best hacker possible and get the most out of the hacking experience that you have created for yourself in your practices.

Chapter 4: Differences in Hacking

There are two basic types of hacking: passive and active. Beyond these two types, there are many different sections that fit into each one and make the difference up in the way that things are able to be hacked and what each hacker is able to do about each thing. There are many different options when it comes to hacking and making sure that you know how to do different types of hacking will eventually help to make you the best hacker possible and will give you a chance at gaining some of the very important skills that come along with hacking. Just make sure that you can do each one of these in a way that works for you.

Passive Attacks

The passive attacks that you do are the easiest type of hacks to start with. They do not require you to do any active work, and you can just set the hack up and sit back while you are waiting for it to happen. Passive attacks are great for both beginners and others because they allow you the chance to take your time setting it up instead of having to set it all up when you are ready to do it.

Replay Attacks

One of the easiest replay attacks to do is to install your software on the computer and allow it to sit for a short period of time. Let it pick up on all of the things that the person does to get into the computer, including putting any keystrokes in or doing anything that is similar to that. You can then allow it to track all of that so that it will be included in it and it will allow you the chance to make sure that you are doing things the right way.

As you are waiting, you can collect all of the information that you need. If you are trying to get a virus off, you should make sure that the software that you are using is able to pick up the different things that the virus may be doing. That could be the key to killing the virus on the computer and getting the system back to where it needs to be. Just be sure that you are able to get that information with your software.

Sitting Ducks

Another great passive attack that you can use allows you to sit and wait for something to happen on the computer. It will allow you the chance to make sure that you are getting the best experience and that you are able to get all of the information that you need on the

51

computer. By waiting passively for changes to be made to the operating system, you will give yourself a way to simply just appear and make things happen with your hack. It will also give you a chance to ensure that you are getting the most out of the attack.

There are several different options for this type of attack. In general, you do not need to worry about whether or not you are local or remote to the operating system or the computer because you can do it all through the back door.

There are many different options that you have for this type of attack, and it will give you a chance to make sure that you are doing it the right way. If you choose the right type of attack for what you want to do, you can get the most out of sitting and waiting to attack.

Active Attacks

As you learn more about the different types of attacks, you will be able to carry out active attacks more frequently. Active attacks give you a chance to make sure that you are getting the most out of them and that you are able to do the most with your different attacks. There are many different things that are included with active attacks, and you can learn from what you have done with passive attacks. Active attacks, though, require you to do more when it comes to your hacking skills.

The biggest difference is that you will need to act quickly. As soon as you make the decision to carry out an active attack, you will need to be ready to make that attack. Whether that means that you need to prepare in advance or just know the codes all of the time that you are going to use, you should be ready to do the active attacks if that is something that you feel you will need to do to make sure that you are getting the most out of the experience of hacking and what it can provide for you.

Masquerade Attacks

Out of all of the different active attacks that you will learn how to do, masquerade attacks are both the simplest and the most popular in the world of active hacking. You will need to learn how to do these if you want to be the best hacker possible and if you want to make sure that you are getting the most out of the experiences that you have. It is a good idea to learn this hack when you are first getting started with active hacking so that you will be able to build from it later on.

The masquerade attack is one where you disguise yourself as a user on the computer.

You would gather the information that you need from the target and replicate it to be able to use it later on. This would allow you the chance to make sure that you are getting the most out of it and that you are going to be able to promote the different things that are included with the experience. You can make sure that you have mapped the targets in each of the different ways so that you can put them back where they belong, and so you can get into the system.

Mapping Targets

The process of mapping targets is perhaps one of the most difficult aspects of hacking and can be different depending on the different situation that you are in and what you are doing with your hacking. If you are going to be an active hacker, you need to learn how to map targets so that you will be able to get into the system. The targets will make a difference in where you go once you have gotten into the computer or the operating system that you are trying to hack.

The target should be something simple — like the password of the computer — once you have learned this, you can often do much more with the computer, change things around, remove files, and add software to keep it from happening again. You can also use the password, or any type of target, to figure out what type of malicious software is on the computer and what can be done about it. Make sure that you know what you are doing and that you are able to add the different options onto it each time that you do something with the computer. Once you have mapped your targets, you should be good to go.

Finding Weaknesses

There is always a weakness in a system. No matter how good the system, how secure or anything like that, there will be a weakness in it and you will have to deal with that weakness. You should make sure that you are able to find the various weaknesses and that you are getting the most out of it. There are many different weaknesses in computer systems — from the way that they are set up to the information that they have on them — that you can make sure that you are getting the most out of.

As you are working to find the weakness, this will allow you the chance to explore the system. Even if you think you have figured out where the weakness is going to be, you may be surprised to find that it is actually in a different location. By exposing the weakness, you will give yourself the best access possible to the target that you are going after. If you are not finding a weakness in the system, you may consider asking someone to help you out so that you can figure out exactly what you are doing with it and where you are going with it.

Testing it Out

After you have figured out how you are going to get into the computer or the specific operating system, you need to make sure that is something that you are going to be able to do. You should check the system, test the weakness, and proceed if there are no problems. Since there are often problems, you should plan your first attempt to be only a test. If it goes smoothly, you can try to do the hack from that point, but it may be harder for you to be able to do.

If you make a choice to continue with the hack, be prepared to do it once you are in. Despite the fact that you were only supposed to be testing it, it is possible to do a high-quality hack from the testing stage. If you are just testing it and you are not able to get into the system, do not give up. Go back and try to find another weak spot. Most systems have several different weaknesses, and you will be able to take advantage of that as you learn more about the different hacks.

Getting into the System

The weakness is the key to opening up the system, but you still need to make sure that you are able to get into the system. It can be hard to be able to get into the system, but once you are in, you should be able to figure out the different hacks that you need to do. Even if the files are locked with a password, it is often the same as what the computer

59

password is so that, as long as you know what that is, you will be able to get to a point where you are getting the most out of the experience, and you are able to include everything that you need on your hack.

Be aware that there may be some things that are installed on the computer that are meant to keep hackers out. Keep that in mind when you are hacking and be prepared to get through a firewall so that you will not have to worry about it once you are in. Hacking a firewall is nearly as simple as getting into a computer, and it can almost always be done as long as you have mapped your target appropriately.

Learning New Hacks

Once you have learned passive attacks, you should then move onto active attacks. Once you have learned active attacks, you need to keep learning as many new ones as you want. This can be anything from old to new to passive or even active, and the hacks will be many different things. Don't just learn the script for the hacks, but learn the reason behind it and what you can do to make sure that you are getting the most out of the hacking experience.

Try different things to get to the hacking point that you want. Try to learn more hacks and figure out how to do them in a way that makes sense. There are many different ways to hack, and just one of them is not going to make a difference in the different things that you can do. It is important that you learn what you can about hacking and how to write your own codes. Once you have learned how to write your own scripts for hacking instead of just changing around ones that are already made, you will be able to be the best hacker possible and get the most out of the hacking experience.

Chapter 5: Starting to Hack

Learning the basics and the things that you need to know about hacking are important but actually doing it is more important if you want to be able to make it work for you. There are different things that you must know how to do for different types of hacking. Learning what these things are, how to use them and the right way to hack will allow you the chance to make sure that you are getting the most out of the hacking process and that you will be able to truly become a great hacker.

Hacking a Network

The most useful hack is one that allows you the chance to do something in the time that you are normally used to doing it. For example, a good hack is one that you can use both in hacking and in your everyday life, and you should make sure that you are able to use the majority of your hacks all of the time that you are online or in different situations. It is a good idea to try different things when it comes to hacking, and one of the most important things that you should be able to try is hacking a network. This will allow you to get onto a wireless network and get the information that you need.

You will first need to find a program that is able to go back to the roots of the network. You will also need to find a network that works for you and one that will be able to make sure that you are getting the best signal possible. Backtrack into the program to see the specifics of the wi-fi, and you will be able to see the password that goes along with the wi-fi. Write it down and keep track of where you put it so that you are able to use it for a second time. This will allow you to get into the network when you go back to the original after you have backtracked.

Now that you have the password, all you need to do is go back to the wi-fi and select the network. Simply enter the key, and you will be able to use the network. This hack is especially beneficial if you are somewhere that does not have a lot of options for strong wi-fi.

Finding Passwords

There are two ways that you can hack a password. The first way is easy but it requires physical effort, and you must be close to the computer. The easier way for you to figure out what a password is to do it from a remote location that allows you the chance to make sure that you are able to get the password no matter what type of information you are getting. This is a good idea because you don't need to be present at the computer and you don't need to worry about the way that you are going to get to the computer.

The first way is to get to the computer and find the password. You can do this with a program, or you can choose to do it manually so that you are able to get the exact password that you need. The first way to do it is manual. You will just need to watch and see which keys the person puts in to get the exact password. You will then be able to see what they are doing on the computer and what they have saved on it. You can also choose to put a physical software device on the computer. All you will need to do is plug the keystroke logger in for a few minutes, and the computer will automatically pick up on it and allow you to see what the password is the next time that the person types it in. The biggest problem with doing this is that you have to be physically close to the computer to be able to do it and you must make sure that you are getting the passwords without them noticing.

It is much easier to hack into their system from a remote location and download the software onto their computer without having to be in the actual location. Just learn how to get in their system (map the weakness) and enter in. From there, you can learn the password, or you can simply bypass the password to get the information that you need and get into the computer. It will allow you the chance to make sure that you are getting the computer information that you need and you will be able to be included in all of the information on the computer each time that you log on.

Getting in the Backdoor

A backdoor entry into a computer is just a different way of getting into it without having to go through all of the different steps of the process. The "backdoor" is essentially just using something that is similar to a Trojan to be able to get into the program that you want without having to go into the program through the regular way. It is not moral or ethical to use the backdoor on a regular basis, but it is sometimes necessary especially if someone has been locked out of their own computer or something and does not have the actual password that they need to be able to get into the program.

To use the backdoor, you will simply need to create a program that is similar to another program. Make it something that is believable so that nobody will know that it is mocked up. Fill it with the software that you want instead of the software that it looks like and send it to the computer. The person who opens it will think that they are downloading what the program looks like but they will actually be downloading the software that you put into the fake program.

There are many times when you could simply put one type of software into the backdoor through the use of a program, but you could also do it with several of the different software options into the computer. This is the way that you turn your program from a simple backdoor entry program into something that can be used as a Trojan. You should make sure that you are only doing this if you want the computer to have *all* of the options that are included with your Trojan so that you are able to do it the best way possible.

You should always think about what you are doing and whether it is up to your own ethical standards before you use a backdoor entry or Trojan program. This is something that you will need to think about before you have the chance to do more with it and you should decide on whether it is a good idea or not. There are many options that can be used instead of backdoor programs. Always choose this before you choose the backdoor one, because most of these options are much more ethical for you to use.

Replicating the Wi-Fi

If you want to be able to use the wi-fi network without anyone knowing that you are using it, you can just replicate it. You can also do this if you need to create a second network without the need for the first one at all. It will allow you the chance to make sure that things are being done the right way and that you are getting the most out of the different things that are included with the wi-fi passwords. There are many different ways that you can change the way that the wi-fi works and several benefits to it.

The first thing that you will need to do is figure out what the server is for the wi-fi. You can use several different programs to do this, but a good program will allow you to do it all from one single application. It will give you the chance to make sure that you are getting the server information as well as the wi-fi information all from the same location. You should make sure that you include each of the different options with your wi-fi and that you will be able to do more with the wi-fi options that you have.

After you have gotten the server information, all you need to do is replace the wi-fi with the new one. This will require you to choose the one with the strongest signal and replicate it with a new name. The name should look the same as the old one so that people will still click on it but it will actually go to the new network that you created. This will give you a chance to have people on your wi-fi network.

After you have created your new network, there are several different things that you can do. You can learn what people are doing online, you can track their information, and you can even use keystroke loggers to pick up the information that they put into password fields. This will allow you the chance to see that there are differences in passwords. This hack is especially beneficial if you need to find out a lot of information about different people and different users on the Internet because it allows you to pick up on different things. There are not many white hat benefits of replicating the wi-fi but knowing the skill can be useful.

How to Spoof

Perhaps one of the oldest forms of hacking is spoofing. This is creating a website or a program that looks the same as another one and leading the user to a different site so that you will be able to either track their information or steal something that is different from the different options. There are many reasons that you may want to do this, but you will first need to learn *what* it is. By learning the information on spoofing, you will be able to begin doing spoofs and making sure that you have each of the different options included with your spoofing techniques.

Despite the fact that you are going to be able to do different things with spoofing, you should first make sure that you are doing it the right way. The spoof should look exactly like the website, email or text message that you are trying to make it look like. This will allow you the chance to show people what you have done so that you are getting the most out of the situation and so that you are able to include *all* of the information with the spoof. Try your best to be sure that you have made it look the best.

If you want to take the information from the person, you just need a simple form on the site. Make it somewhere that they will go to easily on the safe and that you will be able to enter it into the site. By making sure all of this is going to happen, you will be doing your best at creating a spoof. The person will go to the site or the page and will enter their information in, that information will appear to be on the site that they wanted to go to, but it will actually go to you.

Spoofing is not good for white hat hackers. It is not something that you would be able to use, and you should have a strong ethical code before you try to do it for *any* reason. Just make sure that you are doing it for the right reasons and that you are going to be able to use it for that purpose. While spoofing can also be used just for fun, it is something that you should try to avoid because it is associated with black hat hacking.

Chapter 6: Making Hacking Yours

Hacking can be both something that you enjoy and something that is profitable if you know the right way to do it. There are several different options that you can do when you are a hacker to make money, but the majority of the options that will help you make money with hacking are a great way for you to make sure that you are doing the best job possible. Hacking can be a fun hobby, or it can help you to make some money — the choice is yours and will depend on how much effort you choose to put into it.

Learning the Skills

Learning the definitions of hacking and the various terms that you may come across is one thing but learning how to put this information into practice is something else that is completely different. As you are learning the different terms that are outlined in this book, you also need to learn how to do them. Make sure that you are keeping track of the terms and how you plan to use them and to learn how to make them work for you.

The more skills that you have when it comes to hacking, the more marketable you will be. You should make sure that you are marketing yourself in the best way possible and that you are learning as much as you can about the different things that you can do in hacking. It is a good idea to learn everything that you can, even if it seems like you won't use it at any point throughout your hacking career. As long as you are able to learn things, there is no limit to what you can do with hacking.

Try your best at everything that is related to hacking. Even if it seems like a skill that you will not be able to do or something that you are not good at, you should try your best to be able to learn about it. If you are struggling to learn the different things about hacking or something is not making sense to you, consider asking an experienced person for help. A mentor will always be a good idea when you are learning how to hack. It is a good idea to find someone who can help you and who knows what they are doing.

Quick Improvements

Learning as much as you can about hacking will take some time. It may be hard for you if you have never hacked before or if you have no experience when it comes to hacking. Make sure that you learn what you can about hacking, and this will allow you the chance to make sure that you are doing the most with your hacking experience. You should make sure that you are taking your time, but if you are able to speed things up, you can take advantage of the reduced amount of time that it takes to be able to learn more about hacking.

It is a good idea to try your best and to move forward with different things. The more that you know, the more that you will be able to learn and the more time you will be able to take at learning new things. This means that you should try to make sure that you are learning as much as possible but that you are also doing it in an efficient manner — the less time you take, the more time you have to learn more about hacking and other things that go along with hacking.

A Mentor

Having someone who can help you learn about hacking and the different aspects of it is always helpful, but you should make sure that it is someone who knows what they are doing. Despite the fact that you may think that you can teach yourself, having someone there to check your work as you go will enable you to have a better time with the different options that you have with hacking. Make sure that you learn as much as you can and that you are able to get a lot of experience from the person.

A person who is your mentor will be able to help you understand what hacking does, how it works, and the different codes that you can use when it comes to your hacking experience. The person who mentors you should be someone who knows what they are doing, someone who is patient, and someone who you feel comfortable with each time that you work with them. They will be able to give you a lot of help if they are the right person and they know what they are doing when it comes to the hacking experience.

Helping with Codes

There are many different codes that you need to make your hacking experience better. It is a good idea to write down codes as you learn them. Whether you are putting them into a document or physically writing them down, you will be able to remember them and find them when you are looking for them. It is a good idea to try your best to write down all of the codes that you learn — you never know when you will want to find a great code and you just can't remember it.

You should also learn as much about codes as possible so that you don't have to worry about the different things that go into changing things around. There are many different options for people who want to add more to their hacking background but who do not have that experience. You should make sure that you know codes that you can change around and that you can add to instead of just copying down the codes that you have learned. As long as you are able to learn the codes that allow you the chance to write down different things, you will be able to make sure that you are getting the most out of the experience. It is always a good idea to try your best with codes and try to add to them to see what you are doing.

Despite the fact that you are learning as much as you can about hacking and the codes that go along with it, you will still not know everything that you can about it and about what it means to the different communities that are a part of it. Just trying your best to be able to learn more about codes will give you the chance to learn more, and you will not need to worry about the different issues that come along with coding.

The more that you learn about codes, the more independent you will be with hacking. One of the largest benefits of coding and learning what you can about codes is that you will be able to make sure that you are doing things the right way and that you are writing all of the correct codes. You will eventually go from simple hacks to complicated ones, and you will even be able to design software that will work well with your computer and with other computers.

Protection

Your security is important when you are hacking. While there are many more good hackers than there are bad hackers, you still need to watch out for the ones that are bad and the ones who want to counter-hack you or get into your computer in some way. There are many problems that come along with this, and you should always make sure that you are doing the best job possible from the different options that you have. It is a good idea for you to be able to add more to the way that you do things.

As long as you are working your way toward success, there will likely be some people who will want to bring you down. Keep your mind on these things while you are hacking and to allow yourself the chance to make the right decisions. If you protect yourself while you are hacking, you will not be subject to the attacks that come from other hackers or black hat people who are trying to make things harder for you. Try your best to stay out of the way and don't do anything that could provoke the black hatters to do something to you.

One of the best ways that you can protect yourself is to be a part of a community. You need to find people who are similar to you and who have the same hacking goals as what you have so that they will be able to help you with the different things that you can do. There are many different options that come along with hacking and having a strong community within your reach will give you the chance to make things better for yourself. There are many different problems that may come from not having a community and having a lot of enemies is just one of them that can bring harm to your hacking hobby.

If you are doing everything that you can to be a good hacker and you try to stay out of the way of the black hat hackers, you will not likely ever cross paths with them. You should make sure that you are doing your best to stay around the people who are good hackers and who do not have any interest in black hat tactics. It is a good idea to try to do more with your experience and to do everything that you can with the different options that are included in your hacking community.

Your number one priority, as a hacker, is to protect yourself from malicious hackers.

Looking Ahead

In the future, security on the Internet is going to be much different from what it is today. There will be many different technological advances, and you may not know the things that you are doing for your computer hacking experience. If you work to make sure that you are doing each of the different things in your hacking world, you will be able to learn as much as possible about the different options that are included.

It is a good idea to try to make sure that things are going the right way for hacking. Try to stay up to date on the security that is coming along in the future. Keep an eye out for new security features, not only for yourself, but also for the different hacks that you are going to be able to do. If you want to be able to get into new security systems, it will be much easier to do as long as you have learned the systems and the way that they work.

Hacking and Internet security are no different from the other things that you may have had in the past, and you should always keep up with it. It requires you to maintain different things that will help you learn as much as you can about hacking. Try to follow the trends, learn what you can about different things, and make sure that you are doing your best job possible to ensure that you are getting the most out of the experience. By keeping up to date on security features, you will give yourself the chance to do more and to have more clients along with different hack jobs.

Be sure that you try your best with hacking and with security. There are so many different options that come along with the hacking world and try your best to make sure that you are following all of the security protocols. If you work to make sure that you are getting the most out of the experience, you will be able to learn as much as you can about it. You can make sure that you are getting your hacking security by learning as much as you can about the different options that are included, that are going to be included, and that could happen in the future.

If you have read this book and you are confident in your hacking skills, you need to make sure that you are able to get out and begin hacking as soon as you can. Get the software that you need, learn the different terms, and add the different options that you want to each of the hacks that you are going to do. It is a good idea to start as soon as possible so that you can learn as much as possible from hacking and the things that come along with it.

Conclusion

Thank for making it through to the end of this book, let's hope it was informative and able to provide you with all of the tools you need to achieve your goals, whatever they may be.

The next step is to begin learning the hacking terms, take the time and practice them, and add as much as possible to the different things that you can do while you are hacking. As long as you are working to make sure that you are going to be a good hacker, you will never have wasted any time. Start right away to give yourself the best chance at becoming a hacker in a shorter period of time so that you can truly be ready to become a hacker!

Finally, if you found this book useful in any way, a review on Amazon is always appreciated!